OUR RELATIONSHIPS
ROMANS 9-16

KENNETH SCHENCK

wesleyan
publishing
house

Indianapolis, Indiana

CONTENTS

INTRODUCTION

Paul wrote Romans as he neared the end of a decade-long ministry in Greece and Asia Minor (modern-day Turkey). He first believed in Christ sometime around the year A.D. 33, so the book of Romans came some twenty-five years later as he neared the end of his ministry. Now Paul felt the Spirit calling him west to Spain. He hoped to use Rome as a launching point for a mission there, where the gospel had not yet made a significant impact.

It was in this context that Paul wrote Romans. He wished to introduce himself to the Roman churches and perhaps defend himself against those who condemned his teaching. Accordingly, Romans is the most systematic presentation of Paul's understanding of why non-Jews, Gentiles, could be part of God's people without becoming circumcised and converting to Judaism. Paul may also have heard a few rumors about the Roman churches. He wrote to the Romans with sound advice on how "conservatives" and "liberals" could best get along with one another.

This book presents six weeks of Bible studies on Romans 9–16. Originally, Romans did not have chapter divisions; those were added more than a thousand years after Paul died. I have divided Romans this way for practical reasons, so that this collection of Bible studies covers roughly half of Romans. Following Paul's format, we would group the first eleven chapters as Paul's more theological teaching and the last five chapters as Paul's more practical exhortations.

Each week of this book follows a particular theme and covers a chapter or more of Romans. Within each week, there are five days of reflection on the text, looking at a few verses each day. The first two weeks work through Romans 9–11, the end of the first major section of Romans, its "theological" section. Romans 9–11 have given rise to some major debates among Christians, but we also find some of Paul's clearest statements on how one "signs up" to escape God's coming judgment.

Then the last four weeks work through Romans 12–16, the more practically focused section of the letter. In these chapters, Paul addressed matters that were directly relevant to the Roman churches to which he was writing, matters that also relate either directly or indirectly to our world today as well. The aim of this book is to experience life transformation by studying the words of God revealed to the Romans through Paul. The goal is to hear God speak to you through Scripture and then live faithfully to his Word through the power of the Holy Spirit.

EVERYONE WHO CALLS IS CALLED

Romans 9:1–10:13

"If you confess with your mouth, 'Jesus is Lord,'
and believe in your heart that God raised him from
the dead, you will be saved. For it is with your heart
that you believe and are justified, and it is with your
mouth that you confess and are saved."

—ROMANS 10:9–10

DAY 1

ANGUISH FOR ISRAEL
Romans 9:1-5

INTRODUCTION

In the first eight chapters of Romans, Paul argued that only faith can make one right with God, no matter if one is a Jew or Gentile. In chapters 9–11, Paul mourned Israel's rejection of the Messiah, but he also looked forward to its eventual salvation.

ENGAGE

Paul wanted to make it clear that he did not hate Israel. In fact, if he could have taken the place of those who had not accepted Jesus as Messiah, he would have. He was simply presenting the truth—that his people had not believed. How tragic for this great people with whom God had made such covenants and given the law! These were the people to whom God entrusted the temple, the focal point of his presence on earth. They were the people of Abraham, Isaac, and Jacob, the people to whom God gave such key promises. Even Jesus has his human ancestry through Israel. How unbelievable that God's people by and large had not believed!

EXAMINE

We can translate the second half of Romans 9:5 in two ways. The NIV translates it as "from them is . . . Christ, who is God over all, forever praised!" By contrast, the New American Standard Bible reads, "From them . . . comes the Messiah, who is over all, God blessed forever." Certainly we believe both as Christians. But since the original Greek did not have punctuation, we have to determine which meaning Paul more likely had in mind. Most translations go with the first option, because we as Christians believe that Jesus was in fact God. However, Paul almost never flat out called Jesus "God." In the end, we cannot know with certainty which meaning Paul originally had in mind.

EXPLORE

It is not easy to speak with a prophetic voice among your own people, although certainly some people enjoy causing problems and stirring up controversy. However, this does not seem to be the case with Paul, who did not start out following Jesus and paid a great price when he finally did answer God's calling. Paul's first choice was clearly that his people would believe. He would willingly have traded places with them if he could have. But he chose to be obedient, to be faithful to the message despite opposition, persecution, and accusation. Could you do the same? Are you bold enough to speak the truth in love even when your own family, church, or people might reject you for it?

"Those who think Paul has reneged on his heritage,
Paul would insist, have misunderstood both the heritage and Paul.
Paul's claim is precisely that he is being *true* to his heritage
in taking the gospel to the Gentiles."
—JAMES D. G. DUNN

PRAYER

Father, give me the courage to share the good news of your anointed One, even when it brings opposition from those closest to me.

GOD DECIDES

Romans 9:6-18

INTRODUCTION

The fact that most Jews had not accepted Jesus as their Messiah no doubt put a big question mark over the Christian movement. Paul's answer—similar to those given by other Jewish movements like the Essenes at the Dead Sea—was to see the true Israel as a smaller group within Israel.

ENGAGE

The logical conclusion Paul reached in his argument was that not every Jew was in fact a true Israelite. This conclusion follows naturally from his earlier argument in Romans 2 that circumcision was a matter of the heart rather than of one's outward body. Therefore, the circumcision of many Jews turned out in effect to be uncircumcision, and not every

Israelite was in fact a true Israelite. So why had Israel not believed that Jesus was (and is) the Christ? All true Israel actually had. It was simply not part of God's plan that the rest believe. These are difficult words that seem to conflict with things Paul said later.

"God our Savior . . . desires everyone to be saved and to come to the knowledge of the truth."

—1 TIMOTHY 2:3–4 NRSV

EXAMINE

The idea that God would seemingly randomly decide who would and would not believe in the truth is difficult to say the least. It seems to contradict the idea that God is love or that he is just, as Paul himself recognized (9:14). Two key things to keep in mind are: (1) Paul was trying to explain the fact that most Jews had not believed; and (2) he still thought they would come around (11:11–12). To say that God predetermined much of Israel to disbelieve was an attempt to explain what had already happened. For Paul, it did not indicate what would happen to those same people or impact his mission to them.

EXPLORE

The history of Christian thought somewhat forces us to take sides on the issue of predestination. Has God already determined, as John Calvin taught (1509–1564), who will and will not believe completely as a matter of his determination with us playing no role at all? Alternatively, would God be pleased if everyone believed (1 Tim. 2:4)? Philosophically, the two positions cannot be reconciled, unless everyone is destined to be saved. If we have to pick which position fits the overall spirit of New Testament teaching, the idea that God wants everyone to believe fits better, remembering that Paul did not play out God's determination in the same way Calvin did. Paul's basic point still stands: God knows what he's doing.

PRAYER

Father, give me peace about the mysteries of your will that I do not understand, while resting in the clarity of your love.

GOD IS THE BOSS
Romans 9:19-29

INTRODUCTION

Paul continued to make his emphatic point that God could let the Gentiles into his kingdom if he wanted to and that he was under no obligation to save all the Jews simply because they were Jews.

ENGAGE

In these difficult verses, Paul once more reiterated that God was not obligated to be in an exclusive relationship with the Jews. If God wanted to receive the Gentiles by faith—indeed if he wished to reject Jews who did not have faith and yet were scrupulously following parts of the Jewish Law like circumcision and food laws—he could do so. He was (and is) God. Paul did not word his argument in this way, but this was his basic point. He was explaining to the Romans why God was not obligated to do things the way that seemed clear to most Jews from the Old Testament. His answer was that it was none of their business. God could do whatever he wanted—and still can.

EXAMINE

Paul once again wrestled with mysteries. Didn't God have the right to do what he wanted with his own creation? Paul's answer was an emphatic yes. But to put this question in perspective, we can mention some similar questions. If God is God, can he lie if he wants to? If God is God, could he send Jesus to hell? Most would say either that God cannot because it would go against his nature, or that he simply would not because he chooses not to. Paul was making a strong point here: God can do what he wants. He's God; he's the boss. But these are also unusual verses that we best not make the center of our understanding of God.

"I will plant her for myself in the land; I will show my love to the one I called 'Not my loved one.' I will say to those called 'Not my people,' 'You are my people'; and they will say, 'You are my God.'"
—Hosea 2:23

EXPLORE

Language does many things, only one of which is to make truth statements. The most important question to ask when reading difficult passages like this one in Romans 9 is: What was Paul "doing" with these words and with his predestination language in general? Here it is important to recognize that language of predestination by Paul primarily does two things: (1) it affirms God's authority; and (2) it affirms the special honor of being a believer. In Romans 9, it also tries to explain why so many Jews did not believe. What is crucial to recognize here is that it is always "after the fact" language for Paul. Such language relates to the current state of belief, not the future.

PRAYER

Father, I submit to your authority with my whole heart. I do not need to be convinced of your sovereignty.

ZEAL WITHOUT KNOWLEDGE

Romans 9:30–10:4

INTRODUCTION

In these verses, Paul summed up the takeaway from his arguments in chapter 9. Israel simply wasn't seeking God in the right way, while many Gentiles were. Paul hoped they would come around, although for the moment they seemed to have stumbled.

ENGAGE

Paul reiterated in summation some of the same things he had said throughout the early chapters of Romans. His fellow Jews had focused on the parts of the Jewish Law that most separated Jew from Gentile, such as circumcision and food laws. But ironically, this was not the path to being right with God; faith is—faith in what God has done through Jesus Messiah and faith in Christ as God's king. Christ is the goal of the Jewish Law (10:4), toward which faith points. To try to get right with God by keeping the law is not to rely on God's grace, but to try to demand and earn his approval. It is a path that does not work.

EXAMINE

The fact that Paul hoped Israel would be saved (10:1) reveals that his earlier language of predestination did not function the way many scholars assume. He spoke of misunderstanding and misguided efforts on Israel's part, but he did not focus on God orchestrating these things behind the scenes. His attempt to understand and explain their unbelief did not affect his effort or sense of hope for them. Paul did not connect the rare language of Romans 9 with his practice of ministry or even with his theology elsewhere. He carried out his ministry as if anyone could be saved and salvation could be lost. In fact, as we will see, the heart-hardening of Romans 9 only related to unbelieving Israel and was temporary.

EXPLORE

Paul's critique, that so many of his people had zeal without knowledge, is sobering. Certainly many Christians today seem asleep and lacking zeal. Yet, from another perspective, there is no shortage of zeal to be found in the church. If we think about the Jews Paul was talking about, we can at least understand their perspective. After all, did not the Old Testament seem to consider things like circumcision and food laws important? But the truth of the gospel required understanding beyond the letter of the Old Testament to the spirit and heart of God. Similarly, we must be careful today that love—the core Christian ethic—is always guiding our zeal.

"If God has acted in the Messiah to renew the covenant and create a way of salvation open to all, the focus of any prayer on their behalf must be that they would attain this salvation by the route God had set up."

—N. T. WRIGHT

PRAYER

Spirit, guide my zeal that it will always fit God's purposes and the Great Commandment to love my neighbors and enemies.

DAY 5

EVERYONE WHO CALLS
Romans 10:5–13

INTRODUCTION

So what is God looking for? He wants to give away an innocent status, fully reconciled with himself, for free. All he asks to restore this status is faith in the kingship of Jesus Messiah, a kingship inaugurated when God raised him from the dead.

ENGAGE

The bottom line is that God is only looking for one basic thing to accept anyone, whether it is Jew or Gentile: faith. Anyone who calls on the Lord—anyone, Jew or Gentile—will be saved and escape God's coming judgment. It is not something to be earned or even deserved. It is a free gift. It requires faith in what God has done in raising Jesus from the dead. It requires faith that he is God's chosen king, his anointed Messiah. And that is all one needs to do to become right with God. One need not climb up to heaven or descend down to hell. You can have God's approval simply by confessing Christ as Lord.

EXAMINE

Some features of these verses are lurking beneath the surface. One is the fact that Paul, like the authors of Acts and Hebrews, saw the resurrection and exaltation of Jesus, that he is now sitting at God's right hand in heaven enthroned as a king. To confess Jesus as Lord is to recognize his enthronement when God raised him from the dead (10:9; see also Phil. 2:9–11). It is to confess him as king. Paul also equated calling on the "name of the Lord" with calling on Jesus (10:12–13), quoting Joel 2. In Joel, the name of the Lord is clearly Yahweh, the name of God. So Paul felt comfortable equating Jesus with God— extremely striking in his day.

"Therefore God exalted him to the highest place and gave
him the name that is above every name, that at the name of
Jesus every knee should bow . . . and every tongue
confess that Jesus Christ is Lord."
—PHILIPPIANS 2:9–11

EXPLORE

Romans 10:9 is the last stop on the Roman Road, a series of four verses that explain the need and path to getting right with God (3:23; 5:8; 6:23; 10:9). This verse tells how to "sign up" to escape God's wrath. It is simply a matter of confessing Jesus as Lord, which means to have faith that God raised him from the dead and installed him as King. Of course, to confess someone as lord and king is no light matter. It requires loyalty and submission to the king. It is easy to sign up, but faithfulness thereafter may require great effort, certainly under the empowerment of the Holy Spirit. But it is available to anyone who calls on the name of Christ.

PRAYER

Jesus, I confess you as my king and submit to your lordship. I believe that God raised you from the dead.

BRIDGING PAUL'S WORLD AND OURS

In the Reformation of the 1500s, Martin Luther recognized that some passages in the Bible were clearer in meaning to him than others. He set down the principle that Scripture interprets Scripture, that we should use the passages with clear meanings to interpret the unclear ones. Time has revealed some complications to Luther's method. One is that different Christian groups tend to have a different sense of which passages are clear and which ones aren't.

I suspect that most Christians find Romans 9 rather unclear when it comes to living out our faith. We believe the good news is for everyone. We believe that God loves everyone. It is hard to reconcile these pervasive truths of the New Testament with Paul's argument in this passage. Realizing that the hardened of Romans 9 might still be saved helps as does the fact that Paul specifically had the unbelieving Israel of his day in mind. We may have to wait until the kingdom comes to understand the finer points. Until then, it is best for us not to make this chapter the centerpiece of our understanding of God.

EXERCISE

Examine yourself in relation to the two main takeaways from this week. First, are you submitted to the absolute authority of God over you and every aspect of your life? Second, have you genuinely confessed Jesus as Lord over your life, starting with faith that God raised him from the dead?

THE MYSTERY OF GOD'S WAYS

Romans 10:14–11:36

"Oh, the depth of the riches of the wisdom
and knowledge of God! How unsearchable his judgments,
and his paths beyond tracing out!"

—ROMANS 11:33

BEAUTIFUL FEET
Romans 10:14-21

INTRODUCTION

Paul implicitly justified his mission to the Gentiles. The Jews had already heard, but for anyone who called on the Lord to be saved, he had better take the gospel to the Gentiles, for how would they believe if they had not heard?

ENGAGE

The sequence Paul presented is thoroughly logical. The Gentiles could be saved if they called on the Lord. But they must have faith that God raised Jesus from the dead and that he was Lord before they could call on him. But how could they believe if they had not heard? And how would they hear if someone did not go to them? And those who were to go should have been sent by God as apostles. Paul was such an apostle and hoped the Romans would support him on his way to Spain to take the good news to those who had not heard. They might have faith if they heard, and they would hear if Paul brought them the word about Christ.

"I revealed myself to those who did not ask for me;
I was found by those who did not seek me. To a nation that
did not call on my name, I said, 'Here am I, here am I.'"
—Isaiah 65:1

EXAMINE

Half the passage today is an implicit plea to support bringing the gospel to those who had not heard. The other half laments that the Jews had rejected the message of Christ even though they had heard. Paul was not anti-Semitic here, as we will see with great clarity later. Interestingly, he also treated Israel's majority rejection as their own fault—not as some hardening from God. This highlights the fact that he did not really have as much invested in the predestination language of Romans 9 as some scholars think. Nevertheless, Paul's indictment of the bulk of Israel in his day was strong. "All day long" God had been reaching out to them, but they had not responded (v. 21).

EXPLORE

One issue Christians have debated is what happens to those who have never heard the message of Christ. Did Paul believe Christ would not return until all Gentiles had generally heard to give them a chance? He certainly seemed to sense an urgency to get the message to everyone. Many Christians have taken to heart passages like John 1:9, which speaks of Christ giving light to everyone who comes into the world. John Wesley spoke of God's prevenient grace that comes to us long before we come to him. Many Christians throughout history have accordingly believed that some who have not heard might respond to the light they have sufficiently for God to save them through Christ, even though they do not know him.

PRAYER

Father, make my feet beautiful to all those around me, a reflection of the good news of Jesus Christ.

YOU ARE NOT ALONE

Romans 11:1-10

INTRODUCTION

Despite appearances, God had not abandoned Israel, not least because a portion of Israel believed in Jesus like the remnant in the days of Elijah. More Jews believed than the Gentile Romans might have thought.

ENGAGE

You may remember the story when the prophet Elijah was discouraged because the king and especially the queen were seeking his life. In his self-pity, he was prone to think that he was the only one left in Israel who had remained faithful to God and that everyone else had given in and was worshiping other gods. God assured him that he was not alone, that there were indeed seven thousand others who had also remained faithful. So Paul argued that even though the majority of Israel did not believe, many Jews—including himself—had believed. Paul once again indicated that the current hardness was part of God's sovereign will, part of his plan. He saw the situation as temporary.

> Paul himself was an Israelite, so God obviously had not rejected all of Israel. As in the days of Elijah, God had chosen a "remnant" in his graciousness.

EXAMINE

Paul returned to the difficult theme of Romans 9. It will also become clear further into the chapter that he saw this situation as temporary. Paul was saying that the current hardness of Israel was part of God's plan, but it was only a short-term situation. The way Paul expressed this idea is difficult to process. It might remind us of passages in the Old Testament that speak of God sending an evil spirit on someone (see Judg. 9:23), yet James tells us that God does not tempt anyone with evil (James 1:13). Perhaps the best way to translate Paul's point is that it was more about God's will for Israel to be hardened and less about God causing it.

EXPLORE

Most of us live in contexts where those around us profess not only to believing in God, but also to being Christians. Yet the statistics in these places would indicate that most are scarcely different from everyone else. Indeed, sometimes those who do not believe in God turn out to be more virtuous and loving than those who say they do believe. For those who endeavor to be fully devoted followers of Jesus Christ, it can sometimes feel like even in the church there is none righteous. Paul would have us know that God always has a remnant that is truly faithful. They may not be the most visible in the church, but they are among us.

PRAYER

Father, by your power, include me within the faithful. Despite the faithlessness of others, help me be faithful.

THERE'S STILL HOPE
Romans 11:11-24

INTRODUCTION

These verses reveal the point of all of Paul's comments on predestination. Israel was hardened because God was working with the Gentiles. His plan was to bring in the Gentiles during this phase of Israel's history, after which he would graft Israel back into the tree.

ENGAGE

We now see clearly that Paul's sense of predestination was not that of John Calvin. In Calvin's system, God fixed our eternal destiny before creation, and it is not alterable. But for Paul, even those in Israel whom God hardened were not beyond hope. Their stumbling was a blessing for the Gentiles, perhaps in part because it gave time for the gospel to reach out to all the earth. But their full inclusion would be an even greater blessing (11:12). Israel's rejection opened the door for the Gentiles to be reconciled, and what a resurrection when they would believe (11:15)! God has the power to bring unbelieving Israel back into the family, if they would only believe.

EXAMINE

In *The Princess Bride*, one of the characters says, "You keep using that word. I do not think it means what you think it means." These verses show that Paul did not really believe our spiritual fate was entirely a matter of God's determinism. If unbelieving Israelites would only believe, then they could still be brought back into relationship with God. If the believing Gentiles became arrogant and boasted like the Jews Paul condemned (see 2:17–24), then they could be cut out. In short, when Paul got down to the level of specific individuals, he did not treat the outcome as something God had predetermined. He spoke of salvation as a matter of individual choice and pled with others to make the right one.

Here is the key to understanding Paul's perspective on Israel:
Even those "predestined for unbelief" could come back! This was certainly not the kind of predestination taught in some Christian traditions.

EXPLORE

Two things stand out as takeaways from these verses more than anything else. First, we can never assume that just because we are in God's tree, we don't have to pay attention to being faithful to him. God truly wants everyone to be saved and will take any prodigal back, but he expects faithfulness, and there is no security for those who treat God's grace with contempt. Second, we should never give up hope that someone who has rejected God might one day still turn back. God delights in grafting people back into his tree or into it for the first time. God's delight is to see life from the dead take place!

PRAYER

Father, thank you for grafting me into the tree of faith. I invite your pruning so that I never need to be cut down.

ISRAEL WILL BE SAVED
Romans 11:25-32

INTRODUCTION

Paul made a remarkable claim that the hardness of Israel's heart was only temporary. At the appropriate time, God would forgive their sins, and all Israel would be saved.

ENGAGE

It is hard for many readers to hear what Paul said in these verses because they are so enamored with what he said leading up to this point. Paul said that not everyone in Israel was a part of true Israel. At the beginning of this chapter, he pointed back to Elijah and the idea of a remnant of obedience within Israel. But the train of thought in 11:25–26 is unmistakable. A hardness had come over part of Israel that would last *until* the coming of "the fullness of the Gentiles" (v. 25 NASB).

Then, all Israel would be saved. The transition is from *part* of Israel to *all* of Israel. Accordingly, Paul said those who were hardened would believe and be forgiven.

EXAMINE

With this passage, we see that God in fact wants everyone to be saved. Although Paul used predestination language in Romans 9–11 to explain why most of Israel at the time did not believe, he did not believe it was a permanent situation. It was not that God had predetermined who would and would not be saved from all eternity. Rather, God used the hardness of the majority in Israel to bring the gospel to the Gentiles. Then, when that mission was fully accomplished, God would unlock the hardness of Israel's heart and they would finally be saved. Paul was unclear when this would happen, but perhaps he was referring to the time of Christ's return.

EXPLORE

We find two attitudes toward the nation of Israel today. First, they remain God's special people and the reconstitution of Israel in 1948 was in God's plan. Second, the church has completely replaced Israel for all time. You will not find any legitimate basis in the Old or New Testaments for dismissing the ethnic people of Israel forever from God's plan; his calling is irrevocable (v. 29). Nevertheless, the nation of Israel today does not believe, so it cannot yet be the Israel of promise any more than the Israel of Paul's day. Christians should honor Israel (see Rom. 3:2; 9:4–5) but expect the same righteousness that we expect of any nation.

"'This is the covenant I will make with the house of Israel after that time,' declares the LORD. 'I will put my law in their minds and write it on their hearts. I will be their God, and they will be my people.' . . . 'For I will forgive their wickedness and will remember their sins no more.'"

—JEREMIAH 31:33–34

PRAYER

Father, thank you for forgiving me no matter how far from you I might stray.

OUR UNSEARCHABLE GOD

Romans 11:33-36

INTRODUCTION

Paul ended the first half of Romans in poetic celebration. He and the Romans did not always understand what God was doing, but they could rest assured that he knew what he was doing and that it was glorious.

ENGAGE

In these verses, Paul celebrated the mystery of God's will. Paul reminded the Romans that we as mortals cannot hope to understand all the intricacies of God's plan and purposes in the world. God is God. We will never be able to comprehend the fullness of his wisdom. The decisions he makes will frequently seem puzzling. We would no doubt do many things differently if we were in charge, but God has no counselor who can tell him how to run things better. He is the source of all things, the divine patron who gives more than anyone could ever earn or repay. Nothing happens without his approval. And everything is ultimately for his glory.

EXAMINE

Romans 9–11 include some difficult ideas, as Paul tried to explain not only why the bulk of Israel had not yet believed in Jesus, but also God's full right to do things the way he was doing them. Standing behind Paul's claims that God was in control and that everything happening was part of God's plan was Paul's response to his opponents, among believers and non-believers. A non-believer might have asked how Jesus could be the Messiah when so many Jews had not received him. But even believers might have argued that Paul's focus on the Gentiles undermined God's promises to Israel. Paul answered both in terms of God's right to do things however he wanted.

"Who has a claim against me that I must pay?
Everything under heaven belongs to me."
—JOB 41:11

EXPLORE

When Abraham pled to God for Sodom and Gomorrah, he asked, "Will not the Judge of all the earth do right?" (Gen. 18:25). The answer was (and is) a resounding, "Yes!" We will never understand everything God does or allows in the world. How foolish we must look sometimes when we profess to have God's plan figured out, why he allowed this or that to happen, what he was trying to teach us, or what his plan might be. Ultimately, God's ways are "beyond tracing out" (Rom. 11:33). We cannot know the intricate details of his mind. We must ultimately trust that he is in control, he knows what he's doing, and what he does is right and good.

PRAYER

Father, I praise you for the infinity of your mind's understanding, and I rest in trust of the goodness of your will.

BRIDGING PAUL'S WORLD AND OURS

The question of whether God should have allowed Gentiles into the people of God has long been settled for us, as has the question of whether circumcision and other requirements of the law were necessary to be saved. Over time, the context of Paul's language of predestination and election was lost. The issue came to be interpreted as whether God pre-determines who can be saved and who cannot. But Paul was discussing something quite different. Those in Israel whom God was hardening were not necessarily hardened permanently. Those "out" could still come in, and those "in" might still go out.

In the end, whatever our theory of predestination, we have to live as though anyone can be saved and our salvation is contingent on our faithfulness. The key points are: God can do whatever he wants; we will never fully understand what he is doing; and we are to trust in what he is doing. Even more so, we have faith in what God has already done by raising Jesus from the dead.

EXERCISE

Is there an area of your life where you cannot figure out why God is allowing something to happen? Pray as many times as you need for it to sink in: Father, I surrender to your will; I trust in your goodness; I trust in your wisdom.

RENEWED MINDS

Romans 12:1-21

"Offer your bodies as living sacrifices, holy and
pleasing to God—this is your spiritual act of worship.
Do not conform any longer to the pattern of this world,
but be transformed by the renewing of your mind."

—ROMANS 12:1–2

DAY 1

A LIVING SACRIFICE

Romans 12:1-2

INTRODUCTION

In the first eleven chapters of Romans, Paul set out the gospel. Then, in the second section of the letter, he began to show what the Christian life of believers should look like as they live together.

ENGAGE

The second section of Romans begins with the word *therefore*, indicating that chapters 12–15 are in some way the logical consequence of the first eleven. The first eleven chapters are theology and theory; the last few are ethics and practice. The first chapters present the mercies of God—his grace that reached out to the Romans and declared them right with him. In response, they were to present their bodies to him like they would offer an animal sacrifice, which was (and is) an appropriate act of worship. Like the days of Paul, the world is under the power of sin. Our minds are to conform to a different pattern, one informed by the knowledge of God's will.

> "Paul envisages the sacrifices in question as being physical, indeed animal; but the animals are human, and they are not to be ritually slaughtered but 'presented' to God, still alive."
> —N. T. Wright

EXAMINE

In Romans 6, Paul argued that believers do not let sin rule over their mortal bodies. Here in chapter 12, Paul began to show what such a life looks like. Believers no longer offered the members of their bodies as instruments of sin and unrighteousness, but as instruments of righteous living (Rom. 6:13, 19). Paul used the same Greek word for *present* here in Romans 12 that he used in chapter 6. In Romans 1, Paul spoke of the person who should have known God, but whom God gave over to a "depraved mind" (1:28). By contrast, the believers of 12:2 had a renewed mind, one that knew what God's will was for them and especially how they were to live in the world.

EXPLORE

Paul told the Romans collectively to present their bodies together as a singular living sacrifice to God. There is a corporate dimension to what he said in these two verses that we are prone to miss because our cultures today tend to be so individualistic. The *you* of these verses is plural each time, which fits with the verses that immediately follow. Certainly as individuals we offer our bodies. As individuals we should also have transformed minds. But Paul's focus was even more that we together, as the body of Christ, should demonstrate in our lives together the good, pleasing, and perfect will of God. The verses that follow show what this "spiritual act of worship" (v. 1) looks like in practice.

PRAYER

Father, I offer my whole being to you in response to your mercies on me. I offer you my body and mind.

YOURSELF IN PERSPECTIVE

Romans 12:3-8

INTRODUCTION

These verses give us the first example of what a transformed mind looks like. Such individuals recognize that they are only part of the puzzle, part of a team consisting of the rest of the church.

ENGAGE

In verse 2, Paul urged the Romans to have a renewed mind, which is one set on the Spirit rather than the flesh (Rom. 8:5). The next five verses of chapter 12 show some of the specifics of what it looks like. A renewed mind does not have an overly inflated opinion of itself. It recognizes that while you are incredibly important to God, everyone else in your local assembly of believers is too. God has given you certain gifts, but he has given other gifts to people that you do not have.

They are all gifts from God, not something you can boast about as if you are responsible for your giftedness. So let each person exercise his or her own gifts for the good of the whole body.

EXAMINE

In this passage, Paul gave the Romans the equivalent of what he gave the Corinthians in 1 Corinthians 12, in which his picture of a body with many parts especially targeted a local group of believers in a house church. The local church is the first and most important context for these words in Romans as well. In a local group of believers, there are different kinds of God-given talents and roles. Some are good at seeing the way forward (prophesying). Others are good at informing others about who we are and how we live (teaching). Some are great at encouraging or serving. Some are good at leading. Notice that Paul put this role near the end.

EXPLORE

The lists of roles in Romans 12; 1 Corinthians 12; and Ephesians 4 have resonated with some Christians, particularly in recent decades. You can now take spiritual gift tests to find out what your particular gift is. These tools can be helpful, but they can also feed narcissism and unhealthy introspection. They can turn Paul's instructions about appreciating each other into a mirror to admire ourselves. Paul never meant these lists to be exhaustive or to pigeonhole what God does with you. You can grow; God can change you. These lists are really about appreciating each other and not thinking too highly of ourselves (12:3).

"The body is a unit, though it is made up of many parts; and though all its parts are many, they form one body. So it is with Christ."
—1 CORINTHIANS 12:12

PRAYER

Father, help me to see myself with the proper perspective, as only one member of a body that functions together as one to serve you.

DAY 3

SINCERE LOVE
Romans 12:9-13

INTRODUCTION

Paul's examples of a transformed and renewed mind continue. These verses give a list of virtuous behaviors that should typify the attitudes of believers and the way they live in relationship toward others.

ENGAGE

The specifics of a renewed mind continue. The virtues in these verses are not in any particular order. Some continue the theme of how the Romans were to relate to others. They were to be devoted to one another in brotherly love and honor others above themselves (v. 10). This continues the theme of not thinking of yourself more highly than you should but valuing others as much or more. They were to share with others in their community who were in need (v. 13). Certainly

Paul was not opposed to helping those outside the church, but he emphasized the obligation of helping other believers in need (see Gal. 6:10). Hospitality was a core value of the ancient world.

EXAMINE

Some virtues in these verses have to do with the way we make choices. When we face a clear-cut choice between doing something good and doing something evil, the choice should be easy. We cling to what is good; we firmly turn away from what is evil (v. 9). When we can work for positive change in the world, we make that choice as well. We do not lack in zeal, but advance God's causes with passion (v. 11), remembering the caution of Romans 10:2 that a person can be misguided in his or her zeal. Some things we cannot change. In those cases, we must be patient in affliction, remembering that we have hope (v. 12). We must rely on prayer for change.

"Now about brotherly love we do not need to write to you,
for you yourselves have been taught by God to love each other."
—1 THESSALONIANS 4:9

EXPLORE

Paul's instructions in these verses may seem so obvious that we read over them without absorbing anything. They are easy to affirm and much harder to live out. We might not be able to move past them so quickly if others were assessing how well we practiced them rather than merely affirming them. Do we put others first, or do we make ourselves the first order of business? Do we help others when they are in need and we can help? Is our love sincere? This last admonition moves beyond the motions of love to a heart that is committed to love. Do we love others halfheartedly? They can usually tell. However, in time, motion can produce emotion.

PRAYER

Spirit, change my heart to love sincerely. Start me on the journey in my actions. Then make my heart feel what I do.

LIVING IN HARMONY
Romans 12:14-16

INTRODUCTION

Paul continued to play out what a transformed and renewed mind looks like in practice. It means getting along with everyone, not just those with whom it is easy to do so.

ENGAGE

These verses have something to say about how believers should act in several types of relationships. First, there are those in a less fortunate position than we are, whether they are currently in mourning (v. 15) or of a lower social or economic status (v. 16). We are not to think ourselves better than such people. God does not see it that way and neither should we. Then there are those who oppress us. The human tendency is to curse them, but this is not the Christian approach (v. 14), which insists on looking to the spiritual need of our persecutors. Finally, Paul said we are to strive for harmony in all of our relationships (v. 16).

"Make my joy complete by being like-minded, having the same love, being one in spirit and purpose."
—PHILIPPIANS 2:2

EXAMINE

The last part of Romans 12 reminds us of Jesus' teaching in the Sermon on the Mount, leading many experts to suggest that Paul was passing on Jesus' teaching here. The connection between Paul's and Jesus' teaching is not always clear, and some scholars suggest that Paul did not know much about Jesus or what he taught. In the Sermon on the Mount, Jesus said to pray for those who persecute us (Matt. 5:44), that we are blessed when we are persecuted (5:10–11), and that we are blessed when we mourn (5:4), knowing what is to come.

EXPLORE

Human nature has always found ways around what might otherwise seem to be obvious truths and virtues. One way is to read past things that someone like Paul said because they are so familiar to us. We might read past Romans 12:13 where Paul said to share with God's people who are in need. Similarly, we might skip over Paul's instruction in verse 16 to associate with others no matter what their economic or social status and that we are not to think that we are better than them. We skim over such teachings without stopping to consider whether we actually do them. Or we might think our circumstances give us an exception. Paul gave no exception regarding our attitudes toward others, even if others refuse to live in harmony with us.

PRAYER

Jesus, remind me of your example of blessing those who cursed you and empower me to imitate your attitudes.

LEAVING REVENGE TO GOD
Romans 12:17-21

INTRODUCTION

Romans 12 ends with Paul sharing further instruction from Jesus on leaving judgment to God. When we respond in kind to those who do evil to us, we let ourselves be overcome by evil.

ENGAGE

The connection between these verses and the Sermon on the Mount is clear. Paul said not to repay evil with evil (v. 17). Jesus said not to strike back someone who strikes you and not to refuse someone who takes your tunic or forces you to carry his things a certain distance (Matt. 5:39–41). Paul added an element that is not as obvious in Jesus' sermon, namely, that God will take care of judgment. God is the one who will set things right and remove evildoers from the earth. In the meantime, the Romans were God's redemptive agents in the world. The hope is that, by loving our enemies, they may repent and turn to God.

"But I tell you: Love your enemies and pray for those who persecute you, that you may be sons of your Father in heaven. . . . Be perfect, therefore, as your heavenly Father is perfect."

—MATTHEW 5:44–45, 48

EXAMINE

Paul took a passive view in these verses toward those who do wrong. The idea of revenge was strong in the world of Jesus and Paul. Men were expected to defend their honor and that of their families. Indeed, the original purpose of the "eye for an eye and a tooth for a tooth" rule was probably to keep people from taking two eyes or teeth when you had only lost one. To say that you are not to defend your honor and instead try to save your enemy is astounding. But if everyone always hits back, then there will never be peace.

EXPLORE

Jesus and Paul pushed us to always have a redemptive attitude toward those who do evil. Justice is not the same as revenge. Indeed, discipline is not the same as punishment. Justice and discipline can be redemptive if they are exercised to produce virtue in others, to change lives for the good. Human nature is wired for an endless chain of payback. We will never be able to live at peace with others if we are not willing to put a courageous end to the seemingly endless cycle. Ironically, the idea of justice can become a pretext for us to exact revenge where the punishment exceeds the crime. In such cases, we are actually being overcome by evil rather than defeating it.

PRAYER

Spirit, do the impossible in my heart. Give me the strength and courage to end the cycle of payback.

BRIDGING PAUL'S WORLD AND OURS

Chapter 12 showed the Romans in concrete terms what it meant to present their bodies to God and to have renewed and transformed minds. The key, as we will see even more in Romans 13, is to love one another, not only our friends and those with whom we are on good terms, but also our enemies. Obviously this pattern of behavior is much easier said than done, but the difficulty is no excuse for us not to try.

Indeed, Romans 8 makes it clear that the power of the Spirit is necessary and available to make it happen.

Most of the instruction in the chapter has to do simply with getting along with each other. We live at peace with everyone, including our enemies (12:18). We live in harmony with one another (v. 16). This requires both that we respond appropriately to how others treat us and that we treat others appropriately. It goes without question that Christians should not mistreat others, but do good in the lives of others. The hardest good to do is working for the good of those who do us wrong.

EXERCISE

Reflect on three types of relationships in your life: (1) Do you mistreat others or look down on those of lower status? (2) Do you do good to others when you have the opportunity? (3) Do you act redemptively toward those who do wrong to you? Now make any necessary changes.

WEEK 4

DAYTIME LIVING
Romans 13:1-14

"Dress yourself with the Lord Jesus Christ,
and don't plan to indulge your selfish desires."

—ROMANS 13:14 CEB

DAY 1

GOD ALLOWS GOVERNMENT
Romans 13:1-2

INTRODUCTION

What might a transformed mind look like with regard to governments? For Paul, it largely meant not committing any crimes and giving to Caesar what was his. Spreading the gospel and being ready for Christ's return was far more important than engaging with the government.

ENGAGE

How to get along with the Roman government was a relevant issue for Paul's audience. After all, the Roman emperor Claudius had likely expelled all the Jewish believers from Rome less than ten years earlier. Paul told them it was God's will that the Roman government be in place, since nothing happens in the world without God's permission. Paul put this truth in highly deterministic language, but we can translate his comments in this way: The Romans should be good citizens of Rome because (at least at that time) it was God's will to let Rome govern the world. As Jesus put it, they should "Give to Caesar what is Caesar's" (Mark 12:17).

EXAMINE

Paul's attitude toward the Roman government was similar to that of Jesus. They both considered the Romans irrelevant to their mission. Certainly they both were interested in seeing any Roman soldier or governor believe, but governmental change was apparently not on their agendas. Christians should worry more about each other and the spreading of the good news, and less about secular politics. They should let the world follow its course because that is God's business. They should not take each other to court (1 Cor. 6:1), and they should be concerned about sin in the church, but God will take care of sin in the world (5:12–13).

EXPLORE

For Paul, the Roman government was a given. He did not live in a democratic context where officials could be elected to change the trajectory of the state. He probably also did not think Christ would delay long enough to worry about changing the structures of society. We can wonder whether Paul's principles would ever have led him to support a revolution. Nevertheless, we should not forget that Paul wrote these things at a particular time and place. He wrote elsewhere that if slaves could achieve freedom, they should (7:21). So we can imagine him telling someone in a different time to work for change if God opened the door.

"What business is it of mine to judge those outside the church?
Are you not to judge those inside? God will judge those outside."
—1 CORINTHIANS 5:12–13

PRAYER

Father, give me the wisdom to tell the difference between what I should work to change and what I should accept. Give me the right priorities.

DAY 2

GOVERNMENTS ARE GOOD
Romans 13:3-4

INTRODUCTION

After indicating that God was in control of the governing authorities, Paul actually endorsed governments as instruments in restraining evil and doing good in the world.

ENGAGE

When Paul described the ideal governing authority and what rulers and governmental systems were supposed to do, his primary focus was the restraining of evil. He highlighted the function of governmental authority in stopping criminals from doing wrong. For this reason, believers should not fear ruling authorities because they should not be committing crimes. At the same time, Paul recognized that governments could be God's servant to do positive work (v. 4). Paul no doubt would have commended the Roman authorities if they had fed the poor or in some way embodied "love of neighbor" in their governance. Again, this picture is the ideal of what governing authorities should be. It is thus a proverb to which history provides many exceptions.

"He lifts up a banner for the distant nations, he whistles for those at the ends of the earth. Here they come, swiftly and speedily!"
—ISAIAH 5:26

EXAMINE

It is important to recognize that Paul was not making an absolute statement that has no exceptions. We all know, as did Paul, that governing authorities frequently do evil in the world. Christians have often had much to fear from ruling authorities. Paul himself, ironically, died at the hands of the emperor Nero. How often a Christian should take exception to the general principle of obeying authority depends on what those authorities are demanding. Peter and John disobeyed the Sanhedrin in Acts 4:19 because the ruling authority was telling them to do the opposite of what God required. The general principle is thus to obey those in authority over us except when obedience to God trumps their demands.

EXPLORE

We tend to be skeptical of government. We are not surprised when we find our leaders to be corrupt or incompetent. Paul himself was not ignorant of these things either. Perhaps the most striking thing for us in the verses today is the idea that governments can do good. Whatever we think of public education today, we should remember a time when most children received no education. And no church has the resources to address major disasters in the way so many governments do, despite the fact that many failings also often accompany the help. Even most Christian aid organizations that address issues like world poverty or human trafficking could not survive without some governmental assistance. Governments can do good.

PRAYER

Spirit, give me wisdom in my dealings with the authorities of this world. Help me know when to render to them and when to render to God.

PAY YOUR TAXES

Romans 13:5-7

INTRODUCTION

Continuing with his positive view of governing authorities, Paul instructed the Romans to pay their taxes and give honor to the emperor. They were to be model participants in the society of Rome.

ENGAGE

Paul said that submitting to human authorities was a matter of conscience, even if one did not face punishment for breaking the secular law. Certainly the desire to avoid punishment appeals to our baser instincts. By contrast, the appeal to conscience points to what is actually the right thing to do before God. Here Paul said that paying taxes to the Romans was an obligation, something due to them. Similarly, he implied that giving honor to Roman authorities like Caesar was also an obligation. Submission in this context meant that they willingly chose to conform to the expectations of the secular authorities, except of course when conformity would contradict their faithfulness to God and Christ. Further, Paul said they should respect the authorities.

EXAMINE

Paul's and Jesus' perspectives on secular authorities were similar. Roman governors and emperors would not be in power if God did not allow it. Interestingly, Nero had been a fairly good emperor up to the point when Paul wrote Romans. He would only later be revealed as the nefarious murderer history remembers him to be. Meanwhile, Jesus and Paul focused on such a specific mission that they did not worry about reforming the worldly powers. Paul urged the Romans to blend in and be respectable subjects of the empire. Certainly they would not sacrifice to Roman gods, but they could pay their taxes and pray for the emperor.

"Show proper respect to everyone: Love the brotherhood
of believers, fear God, honor the king."
—1 Peter 2:17

EXPLORE

It is interesting to contrast some of our current attitudes toward taxes and ruling authorities with those of Paul. Surely God wants us to work for change in society if we can. Paul did not see such change as a possibility, and he largely urged believers to accept society as it was. Yet Paul's teaching brings our whining and protesting into proper perspective. Part of the American Revolution was about taxation without representation. Today we not only have representation but police, public schools, and other benefits as a result of our taxes. By contrast, the vast majority of those to whom Paul wrote saw no benefit from their taxes, and they were not represented. We have much to be thankful for.

PRAYER

Father, help me to be thankful for the great privileges I have in my country. May I remember those in the past and present who do not have them.

DAY 4

LOVE FULFILLS THE LAW
Romans 13:8-10

INTRODUCTION

Christians should fulfill their debts with regard to taxes and honor to rulers. What other debt remains? Paul said we have a further obligation to love our neighbors as ourselves, a duty that fulfills the entirety of the Old Testament law.

ENGAGE

The first eight chapters of Romans might leave us wondering exactly what it means to have the "requirements of the law" written on our hearts (2:15), to "uphold the law" (3:31), or for "the righteous requirements of the law [to] be fully met in us" (8:4). Now finally, in these verses, we find what it means to offer our bodies as living sacrifices and to have transformed and renewed minds. The answer is to love our neighbors. It is this one thing that the Spirit empowers believers to do and that we are unable to do without the Spirit's power.

"The neighbor is the person encountered in the course of daily life who has a need which lays claim to the believer's resources—a claim . . . that often has an unexpected quality for which no forward planning is possible."
—JAMES D. G. DUNN

EXAMINE

The New Testament consistently makes love the Christian ethic and God's central command. Jesus taught that it was the greatest commandment (Mark 12:29–31); James called it the "royal law found in Scripture" (James 2:8); John considered love the essence of who God is (1 John 4:8, 16) and made love of our brothers and sisters the best indication that we love God (4:21). Jesus said that we must love our neighbor and our enemy (Matt. 5:44). No one else is left. We are never justified in hating another person. We may try to excuse ourselves in the name of hating sin, but in God's eyes, hatred toward any other human is contrary to his will.

EXPLORE

The love rule is the great clarifier. Christian love is distinct from lust and self-centered desire. Could I steal in this situation? Could I commit adultery in this situation? The question is: Am I operating out of genuine love for all the individuals involved? Does my action harm or wrong others? If you truly love others, you will not steal from them, cheat on your spouse or someone else's, or murder anyone. We automatically keep more than half of the Ten Commandments simply by loving others. And since we show love to God by loving others, we keep the other commandment to love God at the same time.

PRAYER

Lord, do not let me make excuses for hatred, either in my actions or in my attitudes toward others, whether neighbors or enemies.

WEAR JESUS
Romans 13:11-14

INTRODUCTION

The first subsection of Paul's practical teaching comes to an end with these verses that speak of the approaching end of the age and the importance of living with a view to the day that is dawning rather than like the night that is ending.

ENGAGE

Paul's comments in these verses remind me of when he talked about the day of the Lord's return overtaking most people like a thief in the night (1 Thess. 5:1). But believers are sons of light and should not be surprised in that way (5:4–8). Indeed, Paul spoke of having armor on in readiness, just as he mentioned "armor of light" here (Rom. 13:12). In the years since Paul had written 1 Thessalonians, his tone of immediate expectation for Christ to return had softened a little. Nevertheless, that imminence can be sensed here. The day is almost here (v. 12). "Our salvation is nearer now than when we first believed" (v. 11).

EXAMINE

God can use the most interesting things to tug on our souls. The early Christian St. Augustine (354–430) felt a tug while reading about Paul's comments in verse 13 on living like people of the daytime and not in sexual immorality. Augustine was living with a woman at the time, and this verse hit him so hard that he abandoned sex altogether for the rest of his life. Paul likened sexual immorality and drunkenness to things you do at night when no one can see. He hearkened back to his earlier argument when he said such things involve gratifying the desires of our flesh (see Gal. 5:16–21). They are deeds of darkness (Rom. 13:12).

"For all of you who were baptized into Christ have
clothed yourselves with Christ."
—GALATIANS 3:27

EXPLORE

When Paul wrote that the Romans' salvation was closer than when they first believed, he probably did not anticipate we would still be waiting two thousand years later. And yet faith in Christ's imminent return remains a central Christian value. We remain people of the light rather than people of the night. We remain people who are expected to put on Christ and wear him around for the world to see. We remain people who should not gratify our fleshly desires but who rely on the Spirit for the power to live a life of love. The timing of Christ's return remains a mystery, but the ethic we are to live by in the meantime is clear as day.

PRAYER

Father, may everything I do be free of the fear of daytime exposure. May I wear Christ every day and show him to the world.

BRIDGING PAUL'S WORLD AND OURS

Romans 13 continues the discussion of what a transformed and renewed mind looks like, as well as what it means to offer our bodies as living sacrifices. The chapter begins with how we might live in this temporary time under the rule of secular powers like the Roman government. It ends with some Christian basics: the love commandment that sums up what a transformed mind looks like in practice, and a reminder that we must live as though our time is short.

In reality, the time has not been short from our perspective. This fact does not change our obligation to love our neighbors and enemies. It does not change our need to live as people of the day whose deeds do not fear the light. It does not change the appropriateness of submitting to those in authority over us. What it might change is whether we are moved to work for societal change and to change the structures of society. For Paul, working for such change seemed pointless because he lived under the urgency of Christ's immediate return. In Christ's delay, however, we should work to make the world more like the kingdom whenever we can.

EXERCISE

Go through an entire day with this question in mind: Are there ways in which I can work to make this age look more like the day that is coming? Think big, beyond your personal life to your culture at large. Now become an agent of kingdom change.

PURITY OF INTENTION

Romans 14:1–15:13

"Everything that does not come from faith is sin."

—ROMANS 14:23

CONVICTIONS

Romans 14:1-9

INTRODUCTION

In Romans 14 and the first half of chapter 15, Paul dealt with tensions that arose in a local congregation between those who felt free to do certain things and those who did not. In this section, Paul told the Romans not to condemn those with different convictions.

ENGAGE

Christians regularly disagree on what God requires of us, and the early church was no different. Did Gentile believers need to observe the Jewish Sabbath, from sundown on Friday to sundown on Saturday? Should believers who lived in a metropolitan city like Rome have avoided meat from the marketplace, since much of it came from nearby temples? Should they have stopped eating meat altogether like Daniel did? Paul said it was a matter of conviction. Be fully convinced that you are following God's will for you. Life and death are in God's hands, and on such matters we should mind our own business—or rather mind our own relationship with God.

EXAMINE

We will gain a significant insight into the early church if we recognize that the "strong" and "weak" of Romans 14 may all be Gentile believers. We should not think that all those who felt obligated to keep the Jewish Law carefully were Jews and all those who were liberal on such issues were Gentiles. Galatians alone disproves this stereotype, since Paul addressed conservative Gentiles in that letter. Interestingly, Paul did not tell the conservative to stop looking down on the liberal, but the other way around. Those who did not worry about the Jewish Sabbath or eating meat from the marketplace should not look down on those whose consciences would not allow them to do so.

"Whether you eat or drink or whatever you do,
do it all for the glory of God."
—1 CORINTHIANS 10:31

EXPLORE

The problem with convictions is that we tend to disagree on what the debatable and nonnegotiable issues are. Is homosexual practice a matter of conviction or a fundamental? Paul told those who felt free to eat meat not to judge those who did not. He told those who did not worry about the Sabbath not to judge those who did. The problem is that we would not apply this principle to murder or adultery, as if God does not have a firm position on those who feel free to kill others. Such issues are thus matters for corporate wisdom and Christian dialog with the guiding principle of loving our neighbor as the referee.

PRAYER

Spirit, give me wisdom to tell the difference between matters of conviction and matters of unanimity.

DAY 2

ACTING IN LOVE
Romans 14:10-18

INTRODUCTION

Paul was clear that the question of a brother or sister's spiritual destiny is far more important than whether you are right or wrong on a particular issue. You can be right on the issue and yet wrong before God.

ENGAGE

Paul's comments here remind me of other places where he indicated that believers will give an account of their lives before God, just as unbelievers will (2 Cor. 5:10; Rom. 2:6). When the Romans gave their own account, it wouldn't matter what their position was on the question of eating or not eating meat that had been sacrificed. What mattered was whether they acted with conviction in their own actions and lovingly toward others. It is none of my business if my Christian brother or sister does not feel free to do things I do. But it is my business not to lead my brother or sister into temptation and cause them to stumble.

EXAMINE

Paul took a sophisticated position on the question of food. He did not believe that food was clean or unclean—a startling position considering the codes on clean and unclean in Leviticus. What made something clean or unclean was the attitude with which one approached it. We might easily generalize this principle to all Christian ethics. It is not so much specific acts that are right or wrong but a person's attitude in doing them. Acts that are universally wrong, like murder, are thus acts that no one could do anywhere in love. Those who act with peace and joy, as well as love of their neighbor, are the ones pleasing to God (Rom. 14:17–18).

"For we must all appear before the judgment seat of Christ,
that each one may receive what is due him for the things done
while in the body, whether good or bad."
—2 CORINTHIANS 5:10

EXPLORE

How easily Christians get the values of these verses turned around! We are convinced we are right in some belief or practice and then ironically become displeasing to God because of judgmental or hateful attitudes toward others. The irony of what Paul said is that one might actually sin while doing the right thing. I might tell the truth out of hatred toward another. I might use my freedom to behave in a way that causes another believer to stumble. The Christian attitude is thus not one of do's and don'ts or a legally oriented mind. It is one that filters potential actions with a view to their impact on others and the purity of the intentions in relation to God.

PRAYER

Spirit, search my heart. Make my intentions pure toward God and my actions loving toward others, even in my freedom.

DAY 3

FAITH-FILLED CONVICTIONS
Romans 14:19-23

INTRODUCTION

Paul ended the chapter with helpful guidelines on how to act in relation to disputable issues. The goal is peace between each other and actions that build up each other. Basically, we act with faith toward God and love toward each other.

ENGAGE

Everything in the chapter thus far has made it clear that the fundamental principle of conviction is to act lovingly toward each other. We are to act in a way that fosters peace, not conflict (v. 19). In fact, our actions should go beyond the neutral to where they actually build up others. It would be ridiculous to tear down or destroy brothers and sisters over trivial matters like food or drink. Paul went so far as to say that it would be better not to act on our freedom at all than to act freely and harm the faith of others. It is not about my rights, but my relationships.

"Love God and do as you please."
—St. Augustine

EXAMINE

At the end of Romans 14, Paul addressed another lurking issue, namely, that some people claimed that their conscience was clear to do something when in fact it was not. Indeed, a person can be wrongly convinced about what is and what is not debatable. We can condemn ourselves by what we approve. God knows what is really going on. The principle is that we are to truly act out of faith toward God. The overly conscientious should not be troubled by Paul's mention of doubts in verse 23. We are far more introspective than people were in Paul's day. Those who doubt are those who have really strong suspicions that they should not be doing what they are doing.

EXPLORE

Paul's flexible attitude toward convictions may be disconcerting to some, especially since he acknowledged that there would not only be those who confused the universals with the relatives, but also those whose conscience was not truly clear. The key is that none of us fools God on such things. If people's actions are not clearly harming themselves or others, then we had best leave their convictions between them and God. "Whatever you believe about these things keep between yourself and God" (v. 22).

PRAYER

Father, give me strength to trust that you know the truth about other's intentions and that it is not my job to police the church.

DAY 4

A SPIRIT OF UNITY
Romans 15:1-6

INTRODUCTION

The importance of unity of spirit has been in the background of all Paul's instructions about those who feel free to do certain things and those who do not. In these verses, he made this theme explicit. We are to glorify God with one heart and mouth.

ENGAGE

The strong here were those whose consciences did not trouble them when they ate meat potentially sacrificed to an idol or chose not to observe the Jewish Sabbath. The weak were those who were more conservative on these matters. Paul aligned himself rhetorically with the strong, as if these things did not trouble him. Remember, however, that Paul was a master persuader. As he did with the Corinthians, he may have identified with the strong to stroke their egos and disarm them, so that he could convert their sense of superiority into doing the right thing. Hopefully, however, he was able to convince them on the basis of his values—God demands us to build up each other.

EXAMINE

One of the functions of Scripture is to give us encouragement and hope (v. 4). The specific verse from which Paul found hope was Psalm 69:9. The early Christians read many of the verses in this psalm in relation to Jesus' final days in Jerusalem. Originally, the psalm also expressed the plea of someone in deep distress. The fact that the psalmist mentioned his own guilt shows that these words originally had a meaning independent of Jesus (69:5). Therefore, God can not only encourage us from the original meanings of Scripture, but also from meanings the Spirit brings alive through the words. The Bible is a sacrament of divine encounter not only to reveal truths, but also to encourage and change us.

EXPLORE

As with the Philippians, Paul turned to the example of Jesus to point the Romans in the right direction. If anyone had the right to feel superior, he did. If anyone's conscience was clear, his was. Yet he submitted himself to the insults of wrongdoers and was obedient to the point of death (see Phil. 2:8). None of us earned God's favor—Jesus did. If he was willing to forego his rights and authority for our betterment, who are we to cling to what we think we have coming when it hurts our brothers and sisters? Who are we to get up in arms and demand our freedom or rights? In reality, we are nobodies in ourselves. Only Christ makes us something.

"Let the same mind be in you that was in Christ Jesus, who, though he was in the form of God, did not regard equality with God as something to be exploited, but emptied himself, taking the form of a slave."

—PHILIPPIANS 2:5–7 NRSV

PRAYER

Jesus, make my life conform to the shape of your cross as I try to pass on your example of servanthood to my brothers and sisters.

GOD'S GLOBAL PLAN
Romans 15:7-13

INTRODUCTION

With these verses, the second, practical section of Romans comes to an end. Paul celebrated the inclusion of the Gentiles into the people of God with a chain of quotes from the Old Testament that reiterated God's plan.

ENGAGE

Paul returned briefly to the Jew-Gentile issue, expanding on what he said in Romans 11, where he mentioned that the failure at the time for most Jews to believe had opened up a space for Gentiles to come in. Here, Paul said something more radical still. He implied that Jesus would not have had to come to earth as a Jew if it were not for God's promises to patriarchs like Abraham. The ultimate goal, it would seem, was to see the entirety of the world be reconciled to God. God's special relationship with Israel was a catalyst to save the whole world. Now that Christ had come, all the nations could rejoice and all the Gentiles hope in him.

EXAMINE

The passages Paul quoted from the Old Testament demonstrate that Paul believed the inclusion of Gentiles within the people of God was part of God's plan all along. If the audience was primarily Gentile, then Paul here pointed to the grace God showed in accepting them alongside the Jews to argue that they should also accept one another. When Christ came to earth, the Gentiles were alienated from the one true God. Yet Christ came and opened the door for Gentiles to be accepted. It would be inappropriate for the strong among the Gentiles (or Jews) to not accept the weak among them. The bottom line is that they were to accept one another as God accepted them.

EXPLORE

God is present everywhere and in every time. But when he decided to become human, he had to take on particularity. He decided when and where in history to take on flesh—what time, nation, and village. The scandal of Jesus' particularity is that he was a Jewish man in the Roman Empire two thousand years ago in a backwater region called Galilee. Some might be tempted to think these particulars separate him from women, Gentiles, and those before and after him. But the important thing is that he became a servant of the particular—as each of us is—so that he might be a universal savior.

"In that day the Root of Jesse will stand as a banner for the peoples; the nations will rally to him, and his place of rest will be glorious."
—Isaiah 11:10

PRAYER

Father, may I accept others in full recognition that I also was once alienated and needed to be accepted.

BRIDGING PAUL'S WORLD AND OURS

The church today is rife with disagreements over countless issues. We may not squabble over eating meat from a nearby temple, but we have plenty of our own issues. The Christian scene today has tens of thousands of independent groups, each of which thinks that it has some corner on the right answers. Despite the distance in time, Paul's ground rules speak directly to our context as if Paul had written them yesterday.

In terms of our actions, love and edification must be the guiding principle. Does my alleged freedom hurt anyone else? Does it help anyone else for me to exercise my freedom? I must love my brother and sister and leave their relationship with God to them and God. I must accept the person who does not feel free on some issue that I do. After all, God accepted me. He will do the policing of the heart. No one is fooling him.

And I must be careful not to fool myself. I can be wrongly convinced to my own destruction. I can pretend that my conscience is clear when in fact I have serious doubts. In the end, whatever is not faith is sin.

EXERCISE

Reflect on some issue over which you disagree with other Christians you know. Now examine yourself. Have you ever thought yourself superior because of your position? Do you trust God to examine their hearts? Are your own actions full of faith with God and love of others?

SOLIDIFYING RELATIONSHIPS
Romans 15:14–16:27

"Now to him who is able to establish you by my gospel
and the proclamation of Jesus Christ, according to the
revelation of the mystery hidden for long ages past, but now
revealed and made known through the prophetic writings
by the command of the eternal God, so that all nations might
believe and obey him—to the only wise God be glory
forever through Jesus Christ! Amen."

—ROMANS 16:25–27

THROUGH THE SPIRIT

Romans 15:14-22

INTRODUCTION

Paul began to offer some closing remarks to the Romans. He spoke of how busy he had been planting churches around the Mediterranean, how God had worked through him, and how he was ready to come to them.

ENGAGE

Paul gave some key insights into his sense of calling in these verses. First, God had called him as an apostle to Gentiles, rather than to Jews. Even though he did not found the churches at Rome, he felt the authority as minister to the Gentiles to admonish them quite boldly. He even used priestly language in verse 16. As all believers must offer themselves as a living sacrifice to God, Paul, as a priestly liturgist, was offering up the

Gentiles to God as an offering. The Holy Spirit was in a process of setting them apart as holy to God, sanctifying them. Clearly he was excited to minister to them. He gloried in the task and considered them a healthy community of faith.

EXAMINE

A second insight into Paul's calling is his sense that God had called him to be a church planter and missionary. He did not see pastoring the believers of a city for a lifetime as his calling, but he was to establish churches in places where the gospel had not yet reached. He mentioned practically the full crescent of the Mediterranean, from Jerusalem all the way around to the far northwest corner of Greece—Illyricum—a place Acts never even tells us he went. One reason he did not plan on spending too long in Rome was because its churches were already established. But he was excited that after years of wanting to come to them, it finally seemed to be coming about.

EXPLORE

Many of us would love to have the clarity of calling that Paul had. Of course, he probably did not get that clarity overnight. He did not start out as a believer and in fact opposed the Jesus movement quite strongly at first. There was also a period of almost fifteen years after he believed where not much is known about what he did. But Paul had an immense sense of clarity by the time he wrote Romans. We can see a significance to his ministry far beyond anything he could have imagined. In the end, it is ultimately about God and what he is doing with us. We do not really need to know the bigger picture.

"Before Paul began, neither Asia Minor nor Greece had heard of Jesus of Nazareth; by the time he was writing this letter, there were little communities all over that part of Caesar's empire . . . in which Jesus was being celebrated as the risen Messiah, the world's true Lord."
—N. T. WRIGHT

PRAYER

Father, I surrender to your plan for me in your mission, whether I know exactly what that is yet or not.

DAY *2*

JOIN MY STRUGGLE
Romans 15:23-33

INTRODUCTION

These verses give some of Paul's final comments to the Romans, as the greetings of chapter 16 may actually have gone to Ephesus, where Paul had just been. Paul ended by asking the Romans to join his struggle by praying for him.

ENGAGE

Paul asked the Romans to join his struggles by praying for him as he moved forward. He hoped that after he visited with them for a while the Romans would support him as he continued his mission into Spain—a mission he may or may not have accomplished. However, he was more immediately going to Jerusalem, taking with him an offering he had been collecting for some time from his Gentile churches (see

2 Cor. 8–9). He continued to speak of the reciprocity between Jews and Gentiles: The Jews had shared their spiritual blessings with the Gentiles; in return, the Gentiles were to give some of their material blessings for the poor among the believers of Jerusalem.

EXAMINE

Paul's words in these verses are almost haunting. He did not feel any more room to minister in the places he had spent almost the last ten years. He was probably writing from Corinth, a city where he spent several years. If 2 Corinthians 10–13 is any indication, his stay there may have been a little awkward, even as he wrote. He had recently been kicked out of Ephesus (Acts 19). When he passed through on his way to Jerusalem, he avoided the city (Acts 20:16). He was even concerned about visiting Jerusalem, where we knew he would in fact be arrested and imprisoned for several years. He was not even sure the churches there would receive his offering—one that the book of Acts conspicuously never even mentions.

EXPLORE

Paul asked the Romans to join him in his struggles through prayer. This is the great privilege and responsibility we have as a community of faith that reaches far beyond our local church. Certainly we can join in the immediate struggles of those around us. But through prayer, we can also join with those who are suffering far away from us. For as Ephesians says, our struggle is not only with the humans around us but with spiritual forces we can fight directly through prayer (see Eph. 6:12).

"Paul envisaged his time in Jerusalem as his severest challenge yet, a fierce contest in which he might well be the loser."
—JAMES D. G. DUNN

PRAYER

Spirit, bring to mind the struggles of believers around the world. Strengthen me to participate in their fight against the powers of this world.

WOMEN MINISTERS
Romans 16:1-7

INTRODUCTION

Romans 16 may have been a separate letter to Ephesus serving at least two purposes. First, it was a letter of recommendation for a woman named Phoebe. Second, it conveyed greetings to an immense number of people, more than Paul greeted in any other letter.

ENGAGE

The number of women leaders Paul mentioned in Romans 16 is striking. He identified Phoebe as a deacon in the church at Cenchrea (v. 1 NRSV, with the masculine word, not *deaconess*). Cenchrea was a port village of Corinth, the city from which Paul likely sent Romans. Priscilla was mentioned before her husband as one of Paul's coworkers who led a house church (v. 3). Junia, along with her husband, was said to be "prominent among the apostles" (v. 7 NRSV), which makes me wonder if in fact she was a woman apostle who witnessed the resurrected Jesus and was commissioned to take that witness into the world.

EXAMINE

Many experts have wondered if this final chapter of Romans might actually have been a separate letter Paul sent to Ephesus rather than Rome at the same time that he sent Romans. For one thing, this would be an immense number of people for him to know—down to members of individual house churches—at a place he had never visited. After all, he never greeted this many people in any of his other letters. Also, some of the people fit an audience at Ephesus much better than Rome. For example, Priscilla and Aquila (v. 3) were last in Ephesus according to Acts 18 and 1 Corinthians 16, and 2 Timothy has them there later. Similarly, Epenetus was the first convert of Asia (Rom. 16:5).

EXPLORE

We can have little doubt about the fact that most Christian leaders in the first-century church were men. However, recognizing this fact is a far cry from forbidding women to be Christian leaders. The model of both the Old and New Testaments is that God can and does call women to roles of leadership, whether it be Deborah in Judges or Priscilla in Acts. Acts 2:17–18 leads us to believe that such women prophets were a sign that the age of the Spirit had arrived. Whether you want to think of such women ministers as exceptional or now quite regular, it is important not to stand in the way when God calls such women. Paul certainly did not.

"In the last days, God says, I will pour out my Spirit on all people. Your sons and daughters will prophesy, your young men will see visions, your old men will dream dreams. Even on my servants, both men and women, I will pour out my Spirit in those days, and they will prophesy."
—ACTS 2:17–18

PRAYER

Father, move me beyond my stubborn prejudices to see how radically you are working in the age of the Spirit and to welcome it.

DAY 4

WATCH OUT FOR DIVIDERS
Romans 16:8-24

INTRODUCTION

These verses finished the greetings Paul made to whatever location he was commending Phoebe and then perhaps closed the letter to the Romans. We see hints of the people working with Paul at that time and place.

ENGAGE

One of the reasons many scholars believe the bulk of Romans 16 was sent to Ephesus is the extensiveness of the greetings and the intimacy Paul shared with so many. In any case, verses 17–20 may return to Paul's final advice to the Romans. Then, as now, divisive people were always around to create factions. Many of these were good talkers and able to gather a following. Many of them in Paul's day were traveling teachers. Paul had heard good things about the faith of the Romans. He urged them to be wise as these distractors would no doubt multiply. Paul looked forward to the day, which he hoped would be soon, when God would crush Satan once and for all.

EXAMINE

These final verses contain hints of some of the important players in Paul's situation. Timothy was with him as he wrote Romans (v. 21). Gaius, Erastus, and Quartus (v. 23) were probably wealthy and influential members of the church of Corinth where Paul was writing. The entire church of Corinth—perhaps forty to fifty people—probably could fit within Gaius' house (v. 23; see also 1 Cor. 1:14), indicating a fairly wealthy individual. Archaeologists have found a paving stone in Corinth with Erastus' name and office on it, indicating he was a person of some means. Tertius was identified as the secretary who wrote down Romans (v. 22). It was standard practice to use such a secretary, so the picture of Paul sitting down to write is probably not quite correct.

EXPLORE

It would be a useful exercise to pretend that you were away from your local church and writing back to send greetings. A list such as that of Romans 16 would have been read publicly in front of the whole gathering. What would you say about each one, trying to build them up rather than tear down? Who would you thank as being influential in your own personal and spiritual development? Who would you say has been a parental figure to you? Who would you commend for their endurance in faith or the strength of their hope? Who would you push toward future leadership? What would they say about you? What would they think about you?

Almost a third of those greeted in Romans 16 were women, perhaps implying that about a third of the leadership in the church at Ephesus (or Rome) were women.

PRAYER

Father, make me aware of both my strengths and weaknesses, and help me to see the strengths of others.

GLORY TO GOD

Romans 16:25-27

INTRODUCTION

This doxology may or may not have been part of the original letter Paul sent to the Romans. But it beautifully captures the place of Romans within the Christian Scriptures and gives God the glory due him.

ENGAGE

The doxology of Romans is so magnificently powerful that Christians since at least the 200s have passed it along in their copies of Romans. That is, Christians implicitly recognized it as Scripture when they affirmed Romans as part of Scripture. The fundamental point of the doxology is to give glory to God because of his power and will to strengthen believers, and for the mystery of including the Gentiles among those who were saved. This mission to bring Gentiles to faith came by

God's command, which again is something for which we should give him glory. And he has done all these things through Jesus Christ.

> "I am not ashamed of the gospel, because it is the power
> of God for the salvation of everyone who believes:
> first for the Jew, then for the Gentile."
> —ROMANS 1:16

EXAMINE

We have thousands of handwritten copies of the New Testament from the time before the printing press. The earliest copies of Romans have many variations on where certain verses end, and most translations do not even include 16:24. The earliest copy of Romans, for example, has the doxology at the end of Romans 15. Other manuscripts have it twice—at the end of chapters 14 and 16. This variation is another argument supporting the possibility that Romans 16 was originally sent elsewhere. These issues help us keep our priorities in order. What is really important is the message. God apparently was not concerned to give us absolute certainty about the letter or precise words.

EXPLORE

The fact that Paul himself may not have written the magnificent doxology at the end of Romans does not diminish its power. After all, it is not that God cannot inspire anyone but the original authors of the biblical texts—it is just far more difficult to know for sure when he has! These verses remind us that God uses Scripture in far more ways than simply to inform. Certainly everything the doxology assumes is true. But a doxology is about praising God. We participate in these sorts of Scripture. They catalyze our hearts and emotions toward him. When we read Scripture in these ways, we will be much more than informed by revelation—we will be changed more into the likeness of Christ!

PRAYER

Father, change me through the reading of your Word. Play the notes of Scripture on my heart to make a beautiful song of praise to you.

BRIDGING PAUL'S WORLD AND OURS

The last two chapters of Romans point toward a massive network of coworkers, leaders, and faithful believers that God had used Paul to grow and develop. Paul, like all of us, had his strengths and weaknesses. God called him to plant churches where none had ever been before, and he was really good at it because, ultimately, the Spirit blessed his work. But we should not think that Paul did not have some raw natural talents to begin with.

As so often is the case, some of those talents brought weaknesses with them. Paul may have been such a dominating personality that he could scarcely work under someone else. If so, notice how God used Paul's strengths to advance the gospel powerfully while managing Paul's weaknesses. It is sometimes said that that we almost never can completely eliminate our weaknesses. Those who are successful simply learn to work around them or pick an area that does not involve them. These insights not only give us hope, but also insight into how God wants to use us to advance his mission in the world.

EXERCISE

Take a moment to reflect on your greatest strengths and weaknesses. Can you see correlations between the two? Ask God how he wants to use your strengths this week so you can glorify him.

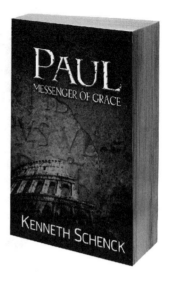

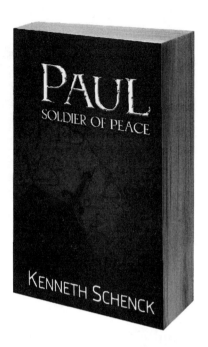

Life Lessons from Paul's Later Letters

Paul went from persecuting the Jewish Christians to battling the principalities and powers so that he could extend their Christian faith throughout the Greco-Roman world. Author Kenneth Schenck delivers more than a narrative recounting of history. Each chapter concludes with the author's insightful reflections of how Paul's life and letters can shape our lives more into the image of Christ. *Paul—Soldier of Peace* covers the later part of Paul's life and ministry including the letters of Romans, Ephesians, Colossians, 2 Thessalonians, 1 and 2 Timothy, and Titus.

Paul—Soldier of Peace
Kenneth Schenck
Price: $14.99
ISBN: 978-0-89827-440-0

wesleyan
publishing
house

www.wesleyan.org/wph or call toll free
1.800.493.7539 M–F 8 a.m.–4:30 p.m. ET